the Ghosts of Zoar ohio

Volume I

Ann Swain
&
Betty O'Neill-Roderick

Published by

INDIAN RIVER
Graphics

Published by

120 West Fifth Street
P.O. Box 605
Zoar, OH 44697
(330) 874-1817
www.indianrivergraphics.com

Printed in the United States of America
10 9 8 7 6 5 4 3 2 1

First printing April 2005

Library of Congress Card Number: 2005921733

ISBN 0-9704760-1-9

Contents

*The Village of Zoar was settled by a group of
German Separatists in 1817.*

Introduction

The Village of Zoar in Tuscarawas County, Ohio, was settled by a group of German Separatists who came to America in 1817 seeking religious freedom. In 1819, they formed a communal society that became one of the most successful experiments in communal living in the United States.

In 1898 the Society of Separatists of Zoar disbanded and the assets were divided among the members. Today the Village of Zoar looks much the same as it did over one hundred fifty years ago. Many of the buildings built by the Separatists are still standing, and the village retains the simplicity and charm of a bygone era. The Ohio Historical Society owns and operates ten of the buildings as museums.

Tales of the German Separatists have been handed down from one generation to the next. Some say they can still feel the presence of these early pioneers who may have decided to make Zoar their home in the hereafter.

The authors operate *Lantern Tours of the Ghosts of Zoar*, where they take guests on a haunted stroll through the streets of the historic village by candlelight. Tours are given at dusk from April through October.⊛

*The Zoar Tavern & Inn was the original home of
the village doctor, Clemens Briel.*

The Zoar Tavern & Inn

The Zoar Tavern was built as House Number 23, the original home of the village doctor, Clemens Briel. Later it was converted into a tavern, along with an adjoining house, and today guests enjoy the casual atmosphere, with great food and sumptuous desserts. Private banquet and conference facilities connect the two houses.

In addition to a great dining experience, upstairs the Zoar Tavern offers lodging in one of their antique-filled guest rooms. The rooms are quaint with hand-hewn beams, and brick and stone walls. But some guests report ghostly happenings like rocking chairs that continue to rock all through the night.

Other guests have awakened to find their furniture has been moved around during the night, while other guests reported they were awakened by the sound of pots and pans rattling in the kitchen, long before the chef began preparations for breakfast.

The restaurant is decorated with photos and artifacts from the Zoar Society of Separatists. One overnight guest came down to breakfast and asked, "Who are the people in that photograph?" No one knew, so he asked to have the picture frame taken apart to see if there were any names written on the back of the picture. When the hostess inquired why he was so interested in the people in the photo, he told her they had visited him in his room the previous night, even sitting down on his bed. ✸

The Zoar Hotel was visited by many rich and famous people during its heyday.

The Zoar Hotel

There are many ghosts who make their presence known in and around the old Zoar Hotel, built by the German Separatists in 1833.

Many rich and famous people visited the hotel in its heyday, including President William McKinley, who often dined at the hotel on a Sunday afternoon.

Today the hotel looks deserted, awaiting restoration as a Visitors Center, however, on quiet summer nights the sound of a great party sometimes emanates from the empty rooms. Lights flicker, and then grow dim, laughter, music and the sound of glasses tinkling echoes through the empty rooms.

Over the years children playing in the village heard the sound of a baby crying in an upstairs room, the cry so plaintive they insisted the village sheriff check the upstairs rooms, they were sure a baby had been abandoned there. But no baby was ever found and the hotel was empty.

In one upstairs room a cradle rocks mysteriously. The hand that rocks the cradle, could it be Mary Ruof's hand? She came to live and work at the hotel at the age of 17, after growing up in the girl's dormitory. She rocked many cradles, raising her four children at the hotel, while also helping with the day-to-day operations.

After her husband, Benjamin Ruof, died of diphtheria, leaving her with two small children, she married his half-brother, Christian, and their union was blessed with two more children. Affectionately called "Mother Ruof" by hotel guests because of her motherly ways, she continued to work at the hotel until her death in 1919. In fact, the Ruof family was given the hotel as their share of the assets of the Separatists Society at the time of the dissolution. They continued to operate the hotel well into the 1920's and they were the last people to successfully operate the hotel.

Although it has changed hands several times, no one has been able to return the hotel to its former glory. Some people say the hotel is cursed, and it is often blamed for the break-up of the society, since it brought in many outside visitors. The Ohio Historical Society purchased the hotel in 1996, and plans to turn it into their Visitors Center, until then the sound of late night parties continues to invade the night sky. ✹

"...on quiet summer nights, the sound of a great party sometimes emanates from the empty rooms. Lights flicker, and then grow dim, laughter, music and the sound of glasses tinkling echoes through the empty rooms."

*The Hermitage, located near the edge of town,
was Alexander Gunn's "private club."*

Alexander Gunn

Those mysterious late night parties emanating from the Zoar Hotel, could they be the same notorious parties that were held in the late 1800's by Alexander Gunn?

After all, everyone who was rich and/or famous in the late 1800's attended Gunn's parties, including Mark Hanna and William Whitney. Whitney was the man who married Gunn's young lady after she spurned him during his youth because he did not have money.

Although Gunn began life as a poor boy, during his lifetime he amassed a fortune and became one of the wealthiest men in the country. He first visited Zoar in 1879, and he immediately fell in love with this quiet, peaceful village. So this world traveler decided to make his home in Zoar.

Gunn was an enigma to the German Separatists because he was an agnostic. Although he did not believe in God or religion, he did believe in reincarnation, so maybe his parties continue today with his many notable guests under the guise of reincarnation.

For some mysterious reason the trustees of the society accepted Gunn, even though he was neither religious nor was he German. However, his presence was disconcerting to this quiet religious community, and Gunn is even blamed for the break-up of the society. At one time there was even an "Anti-Gunn" newsletter decrying his disruption of quiet village life.

Gunn purchased a cabin called The Hermitage, which still sits near the edge of town, but he lived at the Zoar Hotel, and the cabin became his own private club. His parties at the hotel were legendary. Champagne flowed, and when Gunn threw a party, everyone drank. In fact at times, the chef had a hard time getting dinner prepared and served before he passed out.

But dinner at the Zoar Hotel was only the beginning. After dinner, Gunn and his guests retired to the Hermitage where the parties continued until the wee hours of the morning. Can you imagine all this going on in a quiet community where people rose at dawn to begin their chores?

Gunn invited the trustees of the society to be his guests at these parties, and they accepted, so his presence continued to be a disruptive influence until the Separatists disbanded in 1898.

Gunn died on one of his trips abroad and his remains were returned to Zoar for burial. His friends dug a grave at the edge of the Zoar cemetery. As they worked they toasted this man whom they all loved. One worker toasted a bit too much and fell into the freshly dug grave where he spent the night, only to come crawling out as the funeral procession arrived the next morning. ⊛

"His parties at the hotel were legendary. Champagne flowed, and when Gunn threw a party, everyone drank. In fact at times, the chef had a hard time getting dinner prepared and served before he passed out."

The Zoar Hotel provides the setting for several Zoar ghost tales involving dolls.

Zoar Dolls

During the 1960's a family named Ostergard owned the Zoar Hotel. Mrs. Ostergard dressed a doll in Zoar-style clothing and placed it carefully on the landing of the front stairway. Later she found the doll at the bottom of the steps, standing on the bottom step.

She quizzed the employees, accusing them of moving the doll, but they denied touching her precious memento. Yet every time she placed the doll on the landing it would mysteriously descend the steps and be found on the bottom step, not as if it had tumbled down, but rather standing in an upright position.

Mrs. Ostergard naturally thought someone was playing tricks on her until one day she was all alone in the hotel. She placed the doll in her favorite place on the landing. Later she found that once again the doll had mysteriously descended the stairway and was standing on the favored bottom step. At this point, she gave up and decided to keep her doll on the bottom step.

Dolls have always played a part in the tales of the ghosts of Zoar. One day, children playing inside the hotel decided to place a baby doll in the cradle that was rocking mysteriously in the upstairs room. The doll sat upright and the children bolted from the hotel. They returned with an adult brave enough to retrieve the doll, which lay peacefully in the cradle, rocking gently. ✺

The Cobbler Shop is now an antique-filled bed and breakfast which is sometimes visited by the ghosts of Zoar.

The Cobbler Shop
Bed and Breakfast

The Cobbler Shop now houses an antique-filled bed and breakfast. Guests are invited to step into the past when visiting this beautifully restored 19th century home.

Each guest room has been decorated with original antiques dating back to the early 1800's. Guests sleep in authentic rope beds and keep their clothes in a cherry wardrobe, circa 1850. The innkeeper provides a written history of many of the pieces found in each room. However, she warns guests not to be surprised if there's a knock on their door in the middle of the night. It's just the ghosts of Zoar playing a trick on unsuspecting guests.

Downstairs she operates an antique shop, and the ghosts of Zoar have fun opening doors and moving the antiques, often while she is in the next room. So if you are really daring, you'll spend a night in one of the haunted bed and breakfasts of historic Zoar Village. ✇

The ghosts of Zoar are not just seen in historic dwellings.

A Stranger on
the Road

Late one night, two young sisters were driving back to Zoar on the Goattown Road when they ran out of gas. They were feeling quite grown up since the older sister just recently obtained her driver's license, so they decided to walk back to town.

It was a clear summer night and the moon was shining brightly as they proceeded along Goattown Road. Up ahead in the distance, the older girl noticed there was a stranger also walking along the road. The man was dressed in some sort of period costume with a tall hat, and as he walked he appeared to be reading a book.

Now this was a small town where everyone knew just about everyone else, and the appearance of this stranger was most unusual. However, since she did not want to alarm her younger sister, the girl said nothing. But they did speed up their steps, and after a short time, the man just simply disappeared. Suddenly, the road before them was empty.

After they were home safe and sound, the young girl asked her sister, "Why do you suppose that strange man was reading a book in the dark?" The older girl didn't realize her sister had also seen the man until she described him in detail, including the top hat, frock coat and book.

So if you run out of gas along the road around Zoar, look for a mysterious stranger who can evidently read in the dark!✸

The ghost of the Cider Mill is an old Indian who only makes his presence felt by those who work with wood.

The Cider Mill

The Cider Mill was built in 1863 at the height of the successful communal society that had been founded by the German Separatists. Today it is a lovely bed and breakfast with a gift shop on the first floor. Vernon and Dorothy Furbay are proprietors of the bed and breakfast.

The building has been completely renovated and there's a lovely three-story spiral staircase connecting each level. But visitors can't help but wish the parlor's massive 100-year old brick wall could talk, - - what tales it would tell!

During the days of the Separatists, the Cider Mill building served as a steam-operated mill for the hardy pioneers of Zoar. Since these pioneers wasted nothing, the building was also used as a cabinet shop and residence for the cabinetmaker, who made all of the furniture for the village.

Perhaps that's why the ghost at the Cider Mill, an Old Indian, only makes his presence felt by those who work with wood. Actually, he is a long-standing ghost of Zoar, dating back to the time of the Separatists when he was known as the "Old Injun."

Some said the cabinetmaker made up the ghostly tales to keep youngsters from breaking into the cabinet shop while he was away, but no one in the village could dispute the accuracy of the ghost's predictions.

Once the Old Indian appeared and told the cabinetmaker that the President of the United States had been shot. This was most disconcerting to the Separatists, and of course, this was long before the Internet and the days of "breaking news." It took newspapers about six weeks to arrive in the village.

When the newspapers finally arrived many weeks later, the Separatists were shocked to learn that President Abraham Lincoln had been assassinated.

Over the years the Cider Mill Bed and Breakfast has had several owners, and they've come to believe that the ghost of the Cider Mill only makes his presence known to people who work with wood. Actually none of the Cider Mills' overnight guests have reported any ghostly experiences.

However, Vernon is a carpenter by trade, and sometimes he is awakened in the middle of the night by someone or something tugging on his quilt. This mysterious ghost also sweeps all of the items off the top of the dresser. Keys and loose change fall to the floor when no one is in the room.

Sometimes the Furbays' feel a strange chill in the room, and their family dog becomes tense and growls at unseen "ghosts." This very friendly dog becomes apprehensive whenever the cold chill is felt, as if he senses an unseen presence.

Now the previous owners of the Cider Mill reported "no ghosts." Maybe they were a little disappointed, but then neither one of them worked with wood, so that could explain their lack of "ghostly visitors."

One day the lady of the house was getting ready to go away. She laid out her garments and went in to bathe. When she returned to her bedroom one of her undergarments was missing. She was ready to blame the Old Indian until she came downstairs and found their family dog running around with her brassiere. ✲

"...Vernon is a carpenter by trade, and sometimes he is awakened in the night by something tugging on his quilt, or knocking items off the dresser. Their family dog becomes tense and growls at times when a cold chill is felt in the room."

The Zoar Boys were a group of twelve young men who decided to leave Zoar and join the Union Army.

Zoar Boys

The German Separatists who settled Zoar were residing there during the time of the Civil War. Although the Separatists did not believe in slavery, they were avowed pacifists. In fact, one of the reasons they left Germany was because they refused to serve in the German army, so they were reluctant to participate in America's Civil War.

At the time of the Civil War, you could buy your way out of military service by paying $200 for someone else to go and serve in your place. So while many young men left their homes and families to serve in the Union Army, the young men of Zoar were exempt; their exemptions having been bought and paid for by the Society of German Separatists.

Another reason the Separatists paid for these exemptions was because all of their young men were needed to work in the fields and keep up with the successful agricultural business of the Society. Everyone worked, often the women worked in the fields right along beside the men.

However, as the war went on patriotic feelings overwhelmed some of the young men of Zoar, and twelve of them decided to join the Union Army. They left Zoar one night under cover of darkness and enlisted in the 107th Ohio Volunteer Infantry, a largely German unit, comprised of men from Stark and Tuscarawas Counties. Their families must have known they were going, because each one carried a Psalm in his pocket to protect him.

These young men stayed together throughout the Civil War, and they became known as the Zoar Boys. A book, "Zoar Blue" was written telling of their journeys and adventures during war, and it is still available in area book shops.

One night the Old Indian paid a visit to the cabinetmaker. He informed him that the Zoar Boys were fighting in a fierce, terrible battle. He asked the cabinetmaker to please reassure their families that the Zoar Boys were all right and that they would all survive the battle.

It wasn't until much later when newspapers finally arrived that the Separatists realized their Zoar Boys were fighting in the Battle of Gettysburg. And all twelve Zoar Boys lived through this horrible battle that took the lives of nearly 7,000 men in just three days.

After the Civil War most of the Zoar Boys returned to their homes and were accepted back into the Society of German Separatists. ❈

"One night the Old Indian paid
a visit to the cabinetmaker...
He asked the cabinetmaker to
please reassure their families
that the Zoar Boys were all right
and that they would all survive
the battle."

The Boys Dormitory was where the sons of the German Separatists went to live from the age of 3 until they were 14.

The Boys Dormitory

Dave Winter didn't believe in ghosts. No way, after all, he was an F.B.I. agent and they just didn't believe in such things. Today, after living with the ghosts of Zoar for 10 years, he admits he sleeps with a night-light on.

During his years with the F.B.I. Dave often passed through Zoar on his way to meetings at Atwood Lake. The picturesque village captivated him. As his retirement drew near, he and his wife began to think about where they would spend their retirement years, but didn't have a place in mind.

One day on their way to an antique show, they stopped in Zoar, so Dave could show his wife around the village. She too, was captivated by the peaceful village and when they saw a house for sale, they decided to take a look.

The house was the former Boys Dormitory where the sons of the German Separatists went to live from the age of 3 until they were 14. At that time, they were old enough to have a job and could take their place working in the Separatist Society, and so returned to live with their own families.

The couple toured the house, which needed a lot of renovation, and went on to the antique show. But they couldn't stop talking about the house, they were both drawn to it, and before the day was over, they were mentally placing their furniture in the rooms.

A week later they took another look, and bought the house, deciding to move in right away and begin the restoration. In January of 1992, they moved in with two of their children.

After they moved in, Dave had trouble sleeping. The house seemed to have many strange sounds and odors. Sometimes in the middle of the night he heard the sound of children laughing. Other times, the sound of children crying seemed to be coming from the attic.

Their daughter enrolled at the local high school, and when she told the other students where she lived, they said, "You don't actually sleep there do you? Everyone knows that place is haunted."

By February, Dave wondered what he had gotten himself into. The house needed an enormous amount of work, and there were other things bothering him – doors opened mysteriously, lights flickered or went off without anyone touching them, water would gush from the faucets when no one was in the room, and those strange sounds and odors seemed to be coming from the attic.

So he was uneasy as he began the restoration. The cellar was a spooky old place, with two levels going underground. It was a vaulted cellar, commonly called a rathskellar. Late one night, Dave was cleaning the cellar floor with his back to the wall when suddenly the cellar door opened, then closed and the latch clicked shut. He felt a presence in the room. Someone was watching him, yet he couldn't see anyone else in the room.

Thinking his kids wanted to play a trick on old Dad, he snuck up the back stairs, but found everyone was sound asleep. As he returned to the basement, he realized he was the only one awake in the house. He and who or whatever was watching him. "I am not going to leave this cellar," he announced as he continued his work, but the feeling of another presence persisted. From then on he began to sleep with a night-light on in the hall. "I never slept with a night-light in my life, but to this day, that light is on every night," Dave said.

Other family members also felt a presence in the house. Sometimes after hearing the back door and then the kitchen door being opened and closed, they felt a presence entering the house, but no one was visible.

The third floor attic is a big vault-like room where the boys slept. Removing the floor boards revealed a plethora of things the young boys of Zoar left behind, old 1830 coins, toys, socks, a sewing bird and other artifacts.

Since it was a cold, drafty place, their son and his friends used the attic to lift weights. One day as they were upstairs lifting, Dave was in the second floor hallway when the boys came racing down the stairs as if they had seen a ghost.

"Did you see it?" they asked as a vapor trail came down from the attic and slowly made its way down the stairs to the first floor and out the front door.

In June, their grandmother came for their daughter's graduation. They didn't want to scare her, so they decided not to tell her about the strange things going on in the house.

The guest room is on the first floor and grandmother slept there. The next morning she came out to breakfast and asked, "Who were the people with the crying babies who came here last night?" Of course, no one other than the family had spent the night in the house, but grandmother insisted, "I couldn't sleep for the sound of children crying all night." Only then did they tell her of the strange happenings in their restored home.

Later in the summer, a family friend came to visit, and was also given the first floor guest room. Now this time they all stayed up late telling ghost stories, so she knew about all the strange happenings in the house.

Finally they all went to bed. The friend was just falling asleep when she heard footsteps in the hallway coming toward the bedroom. The bedroom door opened slowly, but she couldn't see anyone there. Yet she felt a presence enter the room. Now the pitter-patter of footsteps started coming across the room, so she did the only thing she could do under the circumstances. She turned her head to the wall and pulled the covers up over her head.

The footsteps kept coming right up to the bed. Now she felt hot breath on the back of her neck. "I've never been so frightened in my entire life," she related. She lay there for a while but knew at some point she had to turn over and face this ghostly presence. So she summoned up all of her courage and turned over, only to come face to face – with the family dog.

The family learned to live comfortably with the ghosts. Are they ever afraid? "No, I think it's just kids having a good time with us," Dave said.

Recently while giving a ghost tour through Zoar, Ann Swain felt an apple whiz by her head and impale itself on a fence. Only problem – she wasn't standing under an apple tree, and there was no one else around to have thrown it. Everyone on the tour decided this was just the kind of prank a young boy would pull, especially from the third floor of the Boys Dormitory. ✹

*Zoar Station, built around 1882 and torn down in
1938, was located at the south end of Park Street.*

A Loving Father

Christina Peterman was the first child born in Zoar after the German Separatists established the village. She grew up as a Separatist in the village, married a doctor and they had two daughters. Their home still stands on the main street of Zoar across from the Number One house.

One of her granddaughters, Christina Kappel, married Lorenz Fritz and they had three little children, two boys and a girl. Their home was right next door to the Peterman home, where it still stands today.

Now Lorenz Fritz was an enigma to the other Separatists because he drank, quite a bit, as a matter of fact. Even though the Separatists enjoyed their German beer, and beer breaks were part of their workday, excessive drinking was not tolerated in the community. But Lorenz was a nice young man, evidently a hail-fellow, one of those people who is known and loved by all who knew him.

As the Christmas season drew near in 1888, Lorenz decided to take the train in to Massillon to buy Christmas candy for their three young children. He rode the train into town, as he often did, purchased the candy and Christmas surprises and made the return trip by train. Everyone on the train knew him, including the conductor and engineer, and he imbibed quite a bit of "Christmas spirits" along the way.

But Lorenz did not come home that night. Evidently this was not an unusual occurrence for Lorenz to stay out all night drinking with his buddies. Christine put the children to bed and she retired for the night. She was awakened later by the sound of a child sobbing. Her middle child, Eugene, had awakened in the middle of night and was crying hysterically in his room.

Christina went into his room to comfort him. "What's wrong?" she asked the hysterical child. "Daddy won't talk to me. Why won't my Daddy talk to me?" Eugene asked.

"Daddy's not here, he didn't come home tonight, now go back to sleep," Christina said. "Yes he is," Eugene insisted, "He's standing right over there in the corner. Can't you see him, he's all wet."

"Why won't my Daddy talk to me?" the hysterical child kept repeating. Christina went over and looked, but she couldn't see anyone in Eugene's bedroom. In fact, she never saw her husband again.

In the spring of 1889, after the ice melted, they found his body in the river. They surmised when the train stopped on a trestle over the river, Lorenz jumped off, thinking they had arrived at the train station that stood just South of Zoar. However, in his confusion, he lost his footing, struck his head on the train trestle, and fell into the river and drowned.

No one on the train realized what had happened, and the train continued on to the Zoar Station. But on his way to the hereafter, Lorenz Fritz stopped to say goodbye to his young son, Eugene, in the second floor bedroom of their home on Main Street. ✳

"'Why won't my Daddy talk to me?' the hysterical child kept repeating. Christina went over and looked, but she couldn't see anyone in Eugene's bedroom. In fact, she never saw her husband again."

The former home of the tinsmith, located next to the tin shop shown above, has been visited by several ghosts of Zoar.

Three Sisters

Three charming sisters purchased the former home of the tinsmith and opened a tearoom and bookstore, appropriately called "Books 'N Things."

After they moved into their new home, all three sisters began to notice strange happenings. Although there were no children living in their home, they heard the sound of children talking in hushed voices. Sometimes the odor of a cigar was present, even though no one had even been in the house to smoke. At first they didn't share their experiences, no one wanting the others to think she had "gone batty."

One sister is an avid coffee lover. She would awaken in the middle of the night to the aroma of coffee brewing. Thinking one of her sisters couldn't sleep, she got up to join her for a cup of coffee.

"It was the aroma of coffee being brewed the old fashioned way by boiling it," she said. But when she got downstairs, there was no one in the kitchen, and the coffee pot was cold.

Another sister kept a stack of children's books on a cedar chest in her room, and she would find a child's rocker pulled up to the cedar chest, and a book open, just as if a child had been reading there.

The third sister often heard heavy footsteps in the attic above her room, and once felt a presence enter her room and sit down on her bed, actually leaving an indention in the coverlet.

For a while they didn't talk about their experiences with the ghosts of Zoar, but eventually they did, and realized they were all three experiencing the same phenomena.

Their niece lived in Texas, and when they told her of their ghostly adventures, she was skeptical, but decided she needed to come up for a visit to see if all three had "gone batty."

The first night she slept in the front bedroom, and was awakened by the sound of voices outside, beneath her bedroom window. They were speaking a strange language, possibly German. She got up and went downstairs and out the front door to investigate, but found no one in the street. All three of her aunts were fast asleep. ✸

"She would awaken in the middle of the night to the aroma of coffee brewing...But when she got downstairs, there was no one in the kitchen, and the coffee pot was cold."

*The Inn on the River was built in 1829 to house
visitors travelling down the Ohio & Erie Canal.*

Inn on the River

George is the resident ghost at the Inn on the River. Today he is the most active of the Ghosts of Zoar, and makes his presence known to guests at this fine dining establishment.

The Inn was first built in 1829 to house visitors who came down on canal boats along the Ohio & Erie Canal. In fact, the Inn was the original bed and breakfast in the area. One of the canal boat passengers felt too sick to continue his journey, so he was taken up to the Inn, where later he died.

Although the good German Separatists didn't know anything about the man, they assumed he was a good Christian and gave him a proper Christian burial right in their own cemetery.

About a month later, a lady came to town claiming to be the man's widow. She said he had money and jewels sewn into the lining of his coat. She wanted his property returned to her.

"Dig him up," she ordered. So reluctantly they dug up the man's body, and sure enough, there in his jacket lining were money and gems that the woman grabbed greedily. She immediately prepared to leave town. When the Separatists asked what should be done with his body, the woman replied, "I don't care what you do with him, I got what I came for." After that, she left town, never to be heard from again.

But soon people at the Inn became ill with cholera. Eventually the epidemic spread throughout Zoar, claiming the lives of over 300 people in a matter of three weeks.

Today we know cholera is spread through contaminated drinking water, but many of the Separatists believed that the cholera epidemic was the result of their desecration of this strange man's grave, and the man's ghost continues to haunt the Inn on the River.❂

"Although the good German Separatists didn't know anything about the man, they assumed he was a good Christian and gave him a proper Christian burial right in their own cemetery."

The resident ghost at the Inn on the River,
George, is thought to be the most active ghost
of Zoar.

George

The ghost of the Inn on the River is named George, and he loves to play tricks on people. He dims the lights, opens or closes the drapes, and once stole all of the salt and pepper shakers and put them in the upstairs room (his favorite haunt.)

Chefs at the Inn tell tales of their adventures with George. One chef used a special dish for a soufflé. One day when he planned to serve the soufflé, he set the dish out and left the room to get the ingredients. When he returned, the dish was gone. He searched throughout the entire restaurant, but to no avail. The soufflé dish had disappeared.

Reluctantly, he went out and erased the soufflé from the chalkboard menu. But when he returned, he found the dish sitting on the counter, right where he left it.

George also likes to rattle pots and pans, or sometimes he takes them off the wall and sends them splattering to the floor. Guests sometimes hear the sound of a large tray of dishes crashing to the floor in the kitchen, but a quick look in the kitchen reveals no broken dishes on the floor or anywhere.

Behind the bar, guests have witnessed hands pick up bottles and place them gently on the floor, alarming patrons who wonder if they might have had a little too much to drink.

Guests dining at the Inn claim to have seen George peering in the window, forgetting for a moment that they are seated on the second floor of the Inn. Or a shadow will pass behind someone sitting at the dinner table, or his feet will be seen climbing the stairs.

Painters remodeling the Inn after a disastrous fire were startled by the sound of a generator being turned on, even though there was no electricity inside the building. Once a painter reported someone tapped him on the shoulder while he was alone painting inside the building. He jumped up, left all his paint and brushes and ran into town; and that was the last time he worked alone at the Inn on the River.

A previous owner of the Inn detested country music so much that he would not permit any country songs in the jukebox. Imagine his surprise on his birthday when he entered the Inn and was greeted by the sound of Patsy Cline singing.

Former chef Jim Rhiel reported when his hands are full George has turned on the water faucets in the kitchen, and once he even turned on the stove. Rhiel also saw a large decorative saber mysteriously removed from the wall by unseen hands.

"Everytime I start thinking there must be a rational explanation for all of the strange happenings, George does something to remind me he's still around." Rhiel said. Once they heard a heavy thump upstairs like a tree hitting the building, but when they went outside to check, no tree had fallen. And the last time they got ready to paint at the Inn "someone" mysteriously moved all the kitchen equipment to the center of the room.

George is a fun ghost who likes to play tricks on people and be recognized, but BEWARE, don't make fun of George. Once a group of diners hired an actor to portray the ghost. The actor smeared flour on his face, and crept around outside peering in the windows and making fun of George. As he entered the dining room to join the revelers a picture sailed right off the wall and passed very close to his head, nearly knocking him out. So consider yourselves warned, "DON'T MAKE FUN OF GEORGE!" ✸

The Bimeler House was the home of Joseph Bimeler, the first leader of the Separatists who settled Zoar.

Bimeler House

The Number One house was once the home of Joseph Bimeler, the first leader of the German Separatists who settled Zoar. It is now owned and operated as a museum by the Ohio Historical Society, as are ten other buildings in the historic village.

The Separatists originally constructed the large, magnificent house as a home for the aged. However, just like the Boys and Girls Dormitories, stern matrons ran the home. The elderly residents complained to their families and eventually refused to live there, returning to live with their families.

So the trustees of the Society gave the home to Bimeler and he lived there with his son and other Separatist families until his death in 1853. Built of red brick in the Society's own brickyards and sandstone quarried in the stone quarry just west of town, the house shows the ingenuity of the Separatists. Even the wrought iron railing was made in the Society's foundry.

The Bimeler House Museum contains many of the artifacts of the Society of Separatists of Zoar and is visited by thousands of guests over the summer months.

One guest noticed a tour guide, dressed in period clothing, standing on the second floor landing. But when he went over to ask her a question, she dissolved right before his eyes.

Another time a guide heard a great deal of pounding coming from inside the house. Afraid that someone from a tour had accidentally gotten locked inside overnight, she quickly got a key and went in to release this hapless person. But there was no one in the house. No tourists, no workers and no other guides. Yet the mysterious pounding continued.

So if you're in Zoar on a hot summer evening, take a walk past the Number One House, people tell us the temperature drops ten degrees in front of Bimeler's home. ✺

"One guest noticed a tour guide, dressed in Zoar clothing, standing on the second floor landing. But when he went over to ask her a question, she dissolved right before his eyes."

On foggy nights, mysterious lights have been reported in the swampy fields surrounding Zoar.

Ghost Fields

Over the years, visitors to Zoar have been baffled by the strange lights often seen in the fields surrounding the Village of Zoar. Being located on the Tuscarawas River, the area seems to have more fog than usual, and naturally the river is often shrouded with fog on muggy summer mornings.

During the time of the Separatists, the field east of Route 212 became known as the Ghost Field after a mysterious light was seen there, frightening the horses and anyone else who happened to be in the area.

Swampy fields exist along Route 212 between Zoar and Bolivar and on foggy nights strange lights reportedly arose above the fields. Since this happened close to Halloween, the people traveling along the road named these strange lights Jack-O'Lanterns.

An astute schoolteacher warned the youngsters to stay away from these lights because if you got too close, an air pocket would form around you that would take your breath away. Well, that certainly served to keep the children out of the swampy fields.

Today the strange lights still can be seen on fall evenings. The mysterious lights could be a reflection, or they could be the work of the ghosts of Zoar just having a little fun. Although they produce an eerie sensation, no one has ever lost their breath, or even gotten close enough to touch the lights, since they seem to disappear when anyone gets close. So when you drive along Route 212 on a late summer or early fall evening, look off in the distance and you, too, may see the haunting lights of the Ghost Fields of Zoar.✳

"Today the strange lights still can be seen on fall evenings. The mysterious lights could be a reflection, or they could be the work of the ghosts of Zoar just having a little fun."

The Zoar Cemetery sits high atop a grassy knoll overlooking the lake.

The Zoar Cemetery

The Zoar Cemetery, known as God's acre, sits high up atop a grassy knoll just northwest of town. The Separatists selected this spot for their cemetery when they first settled Zoar, but it is not known whose death brought about the site selection.

The road to the cemetery formerly led past the brewery, along a tree-lined path beside Zoar Lake. It's a peaceful spot, with beautiful sunsets over the lake. Only the rustle of chipmunks or squirrels breaks the silence.

Joseph Bimeler, who died in 1853, is buried there, along with most of the early settlers of Zoar. When the cemetery was expanded and a second part added, the road was changed, so that today the cemetery is located at the very end of Seventh Street.

An array of wildflowers grew along the old path to the cemetery, and one lonely widow would stop and pick a bouquet as she made her daily visit to her husband's grave. The residents were used to seeing her every day, usually about sunset, slowly making her way along the path.

One day she left a note, "I just can't go on without him, so I've gone to the pond," was all the note said. But the people of Zoar knew what she meant. They quickly rushed to the pond on the eastern side of the village. They drained the pond, but there was no sign of the widow.

Later they found her body in Zoar Lake, and she was buried in the cemetery next to her dearly departed husband. But sometimes at sunset, a lonely figure in black can be seen, slowly making her way along the path that climbs up the hill to the Zoar Cemetery. ❋

"One day she left a note, "I just can't go on without him, so I've gone to the pond," was all the note said. But the people of Zoar knew what she meant..."

Cowger House, one of the original Zoar cabins
built in 1817, is the home of the ghost, PJ.

Cowger House

The ghost of Cowger House is a tall silver-haired gentleman in a bilious purple jacket. We affectionately named him PJ (for the purple jacket.) Cowger House is one of the original cabins built by the German Separatists in 1817. Ed and Mary Cowger operated it as a bed and breakfast for a number of years, and they also served delicious candlelight dinners to guests, sometimes with PJ in attendance.

Ed and Mary did a great deal of renovating before opening their fine bed and breakfast. They first heard about PJ, the cabin's resident ghost, from their neighbors who saw him peering out from an upstairs window. Being a former history teacher, Ed was interested in their ghost. He hoped for a meeting with their resident ghost, but it was Mary who had the first ghostly experience.

One night while working late on the renovations, Ed suggested they call it a night and go home. Mary, who was painting an upstairs room, said no because she wanted to finish painting. So Ed locked all the doors and went home.

A short time later Mary heard the front door of the cabin open. Heavy footsteps crossed the downstairs room and began to climb the steps to the second floor. Mary heard a man's voice call out, "Honey, I'm home."

Mary waited but no one came upstairs. Was she hearing things? Cautiously she peeked out, but there was no one in the hall or on the steps. But it must be Ed, Mary surmised.

He must have returned and gone in to the kitchen, and so he couldn't hear her call.

Mary waited a few minutes, she certainly didn't want to go downstairs. She decided to call their home even though she was sure Ed wouldn't answer because he was downstairs.

Imagine her shock when Ed picked up the phone on the first ring. "Oh, you're there?" Mary asked. "Where else would I be?" Ed replied, "I said I was going home. I'm in bed."

Hearing the alarm in Mary's voice, Ed realized that something was wrong. "Did something happen?" he asked. "Uh huh," was all Mary could reply. "Stay put, I'll be right back," Ed told his frightened wife.

Ed returned to find the doors and windows locked just as he had left them. Although he and Mary searched the cabin, they could find no trace of their "midnight" guest.

This tall silver-haired ghost in a purple jacket has been seen in a number of homes around town, including another bed and breakfast owned by Ed and Mary Cowger, Cowger Manor. This lovely retreat is built around the Separatists' original one-room schoolhouse.

Brave guests are invited to stay overnight here along with at least one of the ghosts of Zoar. There's an unusual potty arrangement in one of the upstairs bathrooms, a two-seater potty house for those who don't like to go it alone.

One day, Ed was getting ready for guests and, as always, put a fresh roll of toilet paper in the two-seater. Now he admitted he didn't fold the edges down neatly as Mary does, but he is sure when he left the room the toilet paper was in place. Later, as he showed the guests to their room, he opened the bathroom door, and found the entire roll of toilet paper unrolled onto the floor.

Another couple staying at Cowger Manor saw a tall silver-haired gentleman in a purple jacket descending the steps in front of them. "What time is dinner?" they called out, attempting to engage him in conversation. He didn't respond or even acknowledge them. When they got downstairs, he wasn't in the parlor or any of the downstairs rooms.

While enjoying a candlelight dinner in the 1817 cabin, the couple inquired, "Who is the other guest staying at Cowger Manor tonight? He certainly isn't very friendly." Mary had to tell them, "You are our only guests at Cowger Manor tonight."

PJ Revealed

A few years ago the Cowgers had a guest from Cleveland who inquired, "Do you have any ghost stories about this place?" Oh boy, did they. The Cowgers told him about PJ, the tall silver-haired gentleman in a purple jacket that sometimes peered out of the upstairs windows.

At the end of the story, all the gentleman could utter was, "Oh my God!" "Don't be afraid," Ed tried to reassure him, "It's only a story."

"But you don't understand, my hair is standing on end," the gentleman continued, "I think that's my father."

His father was a Cleveland physician who loved Zoar and visited frequently during the 1940's. He bought the cabin, which was then known as Zeeb's cabin, and spent quite a few of his retirement years in Zoar.

And the final piece of the puzzle slips into place. On a trip to the Orient, the doctor purchased a bilious looking purple jacket, which he wore around the cabin, hence the ghostly apparition we know as PJ.

When the doctor died, he requested that his ashes be scattered in the center of the Zoar Garden in the area commonly called "heaven," but his spirit remains in and around Zeeb's cabin that he loved so much. ✹

Lantern TOUR of the Ghosts of Zoar

Take a haunted stroll through the streets of historic Zoar Village by candlelight. Hear the accounts of Zoar's resident spirits and visit the sites of the hauntings.

There are several B & B's and restaurants in the area if you need food or lodging. Call the Tourist Information Center at 1-800-874-3542 or Zoar Tavern: 330-874-2170.

**TO MAKE YOUR RESERVATION,
CALL 330-874-2002 or RESERVE ONLINE at
http://www.haunted-ohio.com/pages/lntrn.htm**

Zoar Village